DOES YOUR
TONGUE
NEED
HEALING?

DOES YOUR
TONGUE
NEED
HEALING?

DEREK PRINCE

WHITAKER
HOUSE

DOES YOUR TONGUE NEED HEALING?

Derek Prince Ministries
P.O. Box 19501
Charlotte, NC 28219-9501
www.derekprince.org

ISBN: 978-0-88368-239-5
Printed in the United States of America
© 1986 by Derek Prince Ministries, International

Whitaker House
1030 Hunt Valley Circle
New Kensington, PA 15068
www.whitakerhouse.com

16 17 18 19 20 21 22 23 **W** 18 17 16 15 14 13 12

Contents

Contents

Chapter One

Death or Life?

The title for this study is a question: *Does Your Tongue Need Healing?* As we follow this theme, you may be in for some surprises!

Let me begin by pointing out something very significant about the way in which the Creator designed the human head. Every one of us has *seven* openings in our head, the number in Scripture which often denotes completeness. We have three pairs of openings: two eyes, two ears, and two nostrils. But the Creator restricted the seventh opening to *one*, the mouth. I have often asked people, "How many of you wish you had more than one mouth?" But I have never met anyone who did. Most of us have all we can do to use one mouth properly. This one opening causes us more problems than all the other six together!

If you take a Bible concordance and look up all the words related to that one opening such as "mouth," "tongue," "lips," "speech," "words," and so on, you will be amazed how much the Bible has to say about this subject, and it is with good reason. There is no area in our personality more directly related to our total well-being than the mouth and tongue.

Death or Life?

In the first section of this study I wish to share a number of passages of Scripture which all emphasize the vital importance of the mouth and the tongue. Then, in subsequent sections, I will deal with principles that arise out of these Scriptures. First, we will consider Psalm 34:11–13:

Come, my children, listen to me; I will teach you the fear of the LORD. Whoever of you loves life and desires to see many good days, keep your tongue from evil and your lips from speaking lies. (NIV)

The inspired Word of God offers to teach us, as God's children, the fear of the Lord. I have a series of audio cassettes which point out that there is nothing in all Scripture to which there is attached greater blessing, fruitfulness and assurance than the fear of the Lord. So when the Scripture offers to teach us the fear of the Lord, it is offering something of infinite value and worth. By implication, the psalmist says here that *"life"* and *"many good days"* go with the fear of the Lord. In Scripture, life in its fullness and the fear of the Lord are always associated together. The measure in which we have the fear of the Lord is the measure in which we enjoy true life.

Practically speaking, where does the fear of the Lord begin? It is very clear. The psalmist says, *"Keep your tongue from evil and your lips from speaking lies."* In other words, the first area of our life in which the fear of the Lord will be practically manifested is our tongue and our lips. If we can keep our tongue from evil and our lips from speaking lies, then we can move on into the fullness of the fear of the Lord.

Then, out of the fear of the Lord comes life and many good days. The fear of the Lord, life, good days, and the proper use and control of our tongues and our lips are all bound together. *We cannot really have good lives if we do not control our tongues and our lips.*

Proverbs 13:3 states:

He who guards his lips guards his soul, but he who speaks rashly will come to ruin.

(NIV)

Your soul is your whole personality. It is the real you. This is the area where weakness will be manifested first and where the enemy will gain access first. If you want to guard your soul, you must guard your lips. But if you speak rashly, you will come to ruin. The alternatives are very clear. If you control the tongue, then you have protection; but if your tongue gets out of control and you are not master of your words, then the end is ruin. It is so clear; there are no blurred edges.

The whole book of Proverbs is full of these principles. Consider Proverbs 21:23:

He who guards his mouth and his tongue keeps himself from calamity.   (NIV)

Again, the vital area that you must protect

is your mouth and your tongue. Once again, the alternatives are black and white. There is no gray. If you guard your mouth and tongue, then you guard your soul and your life. You are safe. But if you fail to do that, the alternative is calamity. "Calamity" is a very strong word, and I believe the Bible uses it deliberately. The failure to guard our lips and our tongues will ultimately bring us to calamity.

There are two other passages in the book of Proverbs concerning the use of the tongue which are particularly significant.

A wholesome tongue is a tree of life: but perverseness therein is a breach in the spirit. (Proverbs 15:4 KJV)

Where the King James Version says, *"a wholesome tongue,"* the literal Hebrew says, "the healing of the tongue." This clearly indicates that our tongue can need healing. I believe the tongue of every sinner needs healing. The tongue is one area where sin is always manifested in every life. There are some areas in which a sinner may not offend. But the tongue is one area in which every sinner offends, and *it must be healed.*

"The healing of the tongue is a tree of life." Notice again the close connection between life and the correct use of the tongue. The alternative is, *"perverseness therein is a breach in the spirit."* Perverseness means "the wrong use." The misuse of the tongue is a breach, or a leak, in the spirit.

I remember once being in a service where a visiting preacher prayed for a certain person and said, "Lord, fill her with the Holy Spirit."

But the pastor who knew her said, "Don't, Lord; she leaks."

Many get filled and blessed, but it runs out through their tongues. You must keep a tight rein on your tongue if you are going to contain the blessing of the Lord. It is one thing to be blessed; it is another thing to contain the blessing. The healing of the tongue is a tree of life that brings life to us and to others. It works inwardly and outwardly.

Death and life are in the power of the tongue, and those who love it will eat its fruit. (Proverbs 18:21 NAS)

The alternatives are always so clear. It is

either death or life. They are both in the power of the tongue. If we use our tongues properly, they will be a tree of life. But if we use our tongues improperly, then the result is death; and whichever way we use our tongues, we can be sure we will eat the fruit. Each one of us eats the fruit of our own tongue. If the fruit is sweet, we will eat sweet fruit. If the fruit is bitter, we will feed on bitter fruit. God has ordained it that way.

The tongue is the decisive member. Death and life are in the power of the tongue.

Chapter Two

The Heart Overflows Through the Mouth

Our theme will be made a little more relevant by an illustration. During World War II, I was a hospital attendant with the British Army in North Africa. At one time, I was appointed the NCO in charge of a small reception station in the desert that catered only to dysentery patients.

Each morning the doctor under whom I worked would summon me and we would go on rounds of our patients who were all lying there on stretchers right on the sand. I noticed that every morning the doctor always greeted each patient with the same two sentences. The first one was, "Good morning, how are you?" The second one was, "Show me your tongue."

It was not long before I realized that the doctor paid very little attention to the answer to his question, "How are you?" He always moved on immediately to the next question, "Show me your tongue." When the patient stuck his tongue out, the doctor looked very carefully at it. Then he formed his estimate of the patient's condition, much more from looking at his tongue than from the answer the patient actually gave to the question, "How are you?"

That stuck with me, and later, as I moved on into the ministry, many times it occurred to me that God does much the same with us as that doctor did with his patients. God may ask us, "How are you?" and we may give him an estimate of our condition. But I think the next thing that God says, metaphorically, is, "Show Me your tongue." And when God looks at our tongues, then He forms His own estimate of our true spiritual condition. The state of your tongue is a very sure guide to your spiritual condition.

Now we will apply that from Scripture. Many passages establish the principle that there is a direct connection between the heart and the mouth. Jesus states in Matthew 12:33–37:

> *Either make the tree good, and its fruit good; or make the tree rotten, and its fruit rotten; for the tree is known by its fruit. You brood of vipers* [He's speaking to the religious leaders of His time], *how can you, being evil, speak what is good? For the mouth speaks out of that which fills the heart. The good man out of his good treasure brings forth what is good; and the evil man out of his evil treasure brings forth what is evil. And I say to you, that every careless word that men shall speak, they shall render account for it in the day of judgment. For by your words you shall be justified, and by your words you shall be condemned.* (NAS)

Jesus here establishes the direct connection between the mouth and the heart using parabolic language. He refers to the heart as the tree and to the words that come out of the mouth as the fruit. And the kind of words that come out of your mouth will indicate the condition of your heart. He says, for instance, *"A good man out of the good treasure of his heart brings forth good words; an evil man, out of the evil treasure in his heart brings forth evil words."* You will notice Jesus uses the word *"good"* three times, and He uses the word *"evil"* three times. If the heart is good, then out of the mouth will come words that are good. But if the heart is evil, then out of the mouth will come words that are evil.

In Matthew 7:17–18, Jesus expresses in similar language:

Every good tree bears good fruit; but the rotten tree bears bad fruit. A good tree cannot produce bad fruit, nor can a rotten tree produce good fruit. (NAS)

The nature of the tree inevitably determines the kind of fruit. Conversely, when we see the kind of fruit, we know the nature of the tree. The tree is the heart and the fruit is the mouth. If the heart is good, the words that come from the mouth will be good. But if the words that come from the mouth are evil, we know that the heart is evil. You cannot have bad fruit from a good tree, nor can you have good fruit from a bad tree. There is an absolute, inescapable connection between the state of the heart and the state of the mouth.

We may deceive ourselves about the state of our hearts with all sorts of ideas about our own goodness, purity or righteousness, but the sure and unfailing indicator is what comes out of our mouths. If that which comes out of our mouths is corrupt, then our hearts are corrupt. There can be no other conclusion.

I did educational work for five years in East Africa. One of the tribes I worked with was the Marigoli tribe. I was amazed to discover that the same word in that language meant "heart" *and* "voice." I used to wonder how to determine which one the person meant. Does he mean "your heart" or "your voice"? But as I pondered it, I began to see the real insight in the use of that particular language. In reality, the voice indicates the heart. The voice tells with words what is the condition of the heart. This is the same as Jesus said: you cannot have bad words out of a good heart, and you cannot have good words out of a bad heart.

When we come to God with an estimate of our own spiritual condition, I think God is prone to respond the same way that the doctor did with his dysentery patients in the desert. You might say, "God, I'm a very good Christian.

I really love You, and I go to church." But God says, "Show Me your tongue. When I've seen your tongue, I'll know the real condition of your heart."

I want to illustrate this by taking two prophetic pictures from the Old Testament: the first is of Christ Himself, the Messiah, and the second is of the bride of Christ, the church. Notice, in each case, the feature which is emphasized first and foremost is the condition of the lips and the mouth. Psalm 45:1–2 gives us a beautiful, prophetic picture of the Messiah:

> *My heart overflows with a good theme; I address my verses to the King; my tongue is the pen of a ready writer.* [And then these are the words that the writer addresses to the King, to the Messiah:] *Thou art fairer than the sons of men; grace is poured upon Thy lips; therefore God has blessed Thee forever.* (NAS)

Here is a picture of the Messiah in His grace, His beauty, and His moral purity. What is the first aspect of that beauty which is manifested? His lips. *"Grace,"* it says, *"is poured upon Thy lips."* Then it says, *"therefore God has blessed Thee forever."*

Two very important principles are given here. First, the grace of the Messiah is manifested primarily in His lips. Second, God has blessed Him forever because of the grace of His lips. When Jesus appeared in human form and men were sent to arrest Him, they came back without Him and were asked, *"Why didn't you bring him in?"* Their answer was, *"No one ever spoke the way this man does"* (John 7:45, 46 NIV). The grace that poured from His lips marked Him out as the Messiah.

In the Song of Solomon, there is a prophetic picture of Christ and His bride and the relationship between them. Song of Solomon 4:3 is addressed to the bride:

> *Your lips are like a scarlet thread, and your mouth is lovely. Your temples are like a slice of a pomegranate behind your veil.*
>
> (NAS)

The first feature mentioned about the bride is her lips, *"Your lips are like a scarlet thread, and your mouth is lovely."*

The word *"scarlet"* there indicates sanctification through the blood of Jesus. The lips have been touched by the blood. As a result, the mouth is lovely. Notice that the face is hidden behind a veil, *"Your temples are like a slice of a pomegranate,"* but they are behind a veil. Still, the voice is heard through the veil. The other beauties are veiled, but the beauty of the voice comes out through the veil. The voice is the thing most manifested. In the same chapter of the Song of Solomon, we read:

Your lips, my bride, drip honey; honey and milk are under your tongue, and the fragrance of your garments is like the fragrance of Lebanon.

(Song of Solomon 4:11 NAS)

Notice the two distinctive words used of the tongue of the bride, *"honey and milk."* They are also the two distinctive features of the Promised Land. The beauty of the Promised Land is seen in the bride, and especially in her tongue and in her lips. There is a fragrance associated with these beautiful lips that penetrates the veil. Again, the clear form of the bride is not seen behind the veil, but her voice and her fragrance penetrate the veil due to the beauty of her lips. Her lips are like a thread of scarlet and her mouth is lovely.

Is that true of you and me as followers of Jesus? We need to ask ourselves that question.

Chapter Three

The Biblical Picture of the Tongue

We have considered thus far the direct connection between our hearts and our mouths, as summed up in the words of Jesus in Matthew 12:34: *"Out of the overflow of the heart the mouth speaks"* (NIV). When the heart is filled, it overflows through the mouth, and that overflow tells us the real condition of the heart.

In the Old Testament there are portraits of Christ and of Christ's bride. For Christ the Messiah and His bride, the church, the first feature of the grace of God and the spiritual and moral beauty is their lips and their speech.

We are now going to consider a biblical picture of the tongue itself. The epistle of

James deals at length with this subject. First, consider some very searching remarks James makes about the kind of religion which God accepts and also the kind that He does not accept. James speaks about the kind of religion that is not acceptable to God:

> *If anyone considers himself religious and yet does not keep a tight rein on his tongue, he deceives himself and his religion is worthless.* (James 1:26 NIV)

It does not matter how religious we may claim to be. We may attend church, sing hymns and do all the other things that are expected of religious people. In themselves, all those things are good. We may do all those things, but *if we do not keep our tongues under control, our religion is worthless and unacceptable to God*. May God grant that all religious people would face up to this issue.

On the other hand, James speaks about the kind of religion God accepts. Again, it is different from the practice of the average churchgoer today.

> *Religion that God our Father accepts as pure and faultless is this: to look after*

orphans and widows in their distress and
to keep oneself from being polluted by the
world.   (James 1:27 NIV)

The first positive requirement of pure religion is not churchgoing, or even Bible reading. It is looking after and showing practical love to those who are in need, primarily orphans and widows.

Let me suggest, if you are in any way religious, that you take time to look in this mirror of the Word of God found in James 1:26–27. If you do not control your tongue, your religion is worthless. If you want to have a religion that is accepted by God, it must be demonstrated first and foremost in caring for those who are in need: the orphans and the widows.

I think again about the doctor in the desert when he asked his patients how they felt. He really was not too interested in the answer because the next thing he always said was, "Show me your tongue."

That is really what James is saying in these two verses. If you want to impress God with your religion, the first thing He will say is, "Show Me your tongue." He is going to judge from your tongue whether your religion is valid and acceptable or not.

James uses a number of pictures to illustrate the function of the tongue in our lives. First, James says:

> *We all stumble in many ways. If anyone is never at fault in what he says, he is a perfect man, able to keep his whole body in check.* (James 3:2 NIV)

James is saying that if you can control your tongue, you can control your whole life. You are a perfect man if you can control your tongue. Then he goes on in the remainder of this passage to give some illustrations from the natural world. James 3:3–8 continues:

> *When we put bits into the mouths of horses to make them obey us, we can turn the whole animal. Or take ships as an example. Although they are so large and are driven by strong winds, they are steered by a very small rudder wherever the pilot wants to go. Likewise the tongue is a small part of the body, but it makes great boasts. Consider what a great forest is set on fire by a small*

spark. The tongue also is a fire, a world of evil among the parts of the body. It corrupts the whole person, sets the whole course of his life on fire, and is itself set on fire by hell. All kinds of animals, birds, reptiles and creatures of the sea are being tamed and have been tamed by man, but no man can tame the tongue. It is a restless evil, full of deadly poison. (NIV)

James is bringing out the unique significance and influence of the tongue for the whole course of our lives. The first example he uses is the bit in the horse's mouth. He says, "If we succeed in putting a bit in a horse's mouth, we can turn the whole animal around."

The horse, in the Bible, is usually a type of physical strength. James is saying that no matter how strong a horse is, if you can get control of its mouth with the bit, you can control the whole animal. The horse's strength is brought into subjection through the control of its mouth. The same is true with us. That which controls our mouths controls the whole course of our lives.

The next example is perhaps a little more vivid. He compares the tongue to the rudder of a ship. A ship may be a great structure, but be carried to and fro by the tremendously powerful forces of the winds and the waves. Yet, in that ship there is only one decisive, small piece the rudder. It is the use of the rudder that determines the whole course of the ship. If the rudder is used properly, the ship will arrive safely in the harbor. If the rudder is not used properly, the ship is likely to be shipwrecked.

James says it is the same in our lives. The tongue is the rudder. Our tongues control the course of our lives. If the rudder of the tongue is used properly, we will make it safely to our appointed destinations. But if our tongues are not used properly, we will be shipwrecked.

James also gives the example of a small spark that can start a forest fire. Every year in the United States, billions of dollars of damage is caused by forest fires, and they usually start just the way James says, with a small spark. The Forest Department of the United States has a very vivid poster that says, "Only *you* can prevent forest fires."

That is also true in the spiritual realm. The tongue is like a little spark that can cause a forest fire of vast proportions, causing billions of dollars of damage. Many churches and religious groups no longer exist because one tongue set a spark that burned up the whole thing which could never be restored.

The final example James uses is that of a source of lethal poison. He says the tongue is like a deadly element that can poison us by spreading infection through the whole system of our lives.

Consider those examples again: the bit in the horse's mouth, the rudder in the ship, the spark that starts a forest fire, and a poison that is injected into the life stream. The principle underlying each of these illustrations is the same: the tongue is a small part of the body, but it is able to cause inestimable damage that might never be undone.

James goes on to point out, once more, the inconsistencies of religious people:

With the tongue we praise our Lord and Father, and with it we curse men, who have been made in God's likeness. Out of the same mouth come praise and cursing. My brothers, this should not be. Can both fresh water and salt water flow from the same spring? My brothers, can a fig tree bear olives, or a grapevine bear figs? Neither can a salt spring produce fresh water.

(James 3:9–12 NIV)

James is saying exactly the same thing Jesus said. If the tree is good, the fruit will be good. If you have a fig tree in your heart, you will get figs out of your mouth. But if you have a vine in your heart, you will never get figs out of your mouth. What comes out of your mouth indicates what is in your heart.

It is the same, he said, with the flow of water. If the water that comes out of your mouth is fresh, then the spring that is in your heart is fresh. But if the water that comes out of your mouth is salty and brackish, then the spring of your heart is salty and brackish. So that which comes out of the mouth inevitably indicates the true condition of the heart.

Chapter Four

Words Determine Destiny

The essence of the different pictures that James uses to illustrate the function of the tongue in our lives is the same: the tongue is something small in itself, but capable of causing incalculable harm if left unchecked. Of the four particular pictures that I referred to (the bit in the horse's mouth, the rudder in the ship, a spark that starts a forest fire, and a source of poison that corrupts the whole life stream), the one that best illustrates the tremendous potential of the tongue is that of the rudder in the ship.

The rudder is visually just a small part of the ship that is down below the surface. You do not see it when you look at the ship sailing on the surface of the water. Yet that small part, which is not normally visible to the eye, determines the direction of the ship. If the rudder is used correctly, the ship will make it safely to its destined harbor. But if the rudder is misused, almost certainly the ship will suffer shipwreck. The rudder determines the course and the destiny of the entire ship.

The Bible says the tongue is like that in our bodies. When we look at people from outward appearances, normally we do not even see their tongues. Yet that small, unnoticed member is just like the rudder in the ship. The tongue's use determines the course of the person's life. It determines his or her destiny.

To continue our study, we want to consider an example from the history of Israel that drives home this lesson with inescapable clarity. The lesson to learn is this: *Men determine their own destinies by the way they use their tongues.*

The incident we are going to look at is found in the book of Numbers, chapters 13 and 14. The Israelites had come out of Egypt and were on their way to the Promised Land.

God arranged with Moses to send twelve men ahead of them to spy out the land: to find out its general character, the nature of the inhabitants, the kind of cities, the kind of fruit, and to bring back a report. One leader was chosen from each of the twelve tribes to go ahead into the land. They spent forty days walking through the land and then they came back with their report. The report they brought back is given to us in Numbers 13:26–28:

And they [the twelve spies] *went and came to Moses, and to Aaron, and to all the congregation of the children of Israel, unto the wilderness of Paran, to Kadesh; and brought back word unto them, and unto all the congregation, and shewed them the fruit of the land. And they told him, and said, We came unto the land whither thou sentest us, and surely it floweth with milk and honey; and this is the fruit of it.* [The fruit was so heavy that it took two men to carry one bunch of grapes on a staff between them.] *Nevertheless the people be strong that dwell in the land, and the cities are walled, and very great: and moreover we saw the children of Anak* [the giants] *there.* (KJV)

When God gives you a promise, are you going to accept the promise at its face value, or are you going to accept it and then say *"nevertheless"*? That was a fatal word that caused the people to be disturbed and distressed.

Two of the spies, however, Caleb and Joshua, refused to go along with this negative attitude. In Numbers 13:30–31, we read this:

And Caleb stilled the people before Moses, and said, Let us go up at once, and possess it; for we are well able to overcome it. But the men that went up with him said, We be not able to go up against the people; for they are stronger than we. (KJV)

Let us take notice of the words that were used. Caleb said, *"We are well able to overcome it."* The other ten spies said, "We be not able." One set of spies said the positive: "We are able." The other set said the negative: "We are not able." As you follow the story, you will see that each group got exactly what they said. Each group's destiny was settled by their words.

And the LORD said, I have pardoned according to thy word: but as truly as I live, all the earth shall be filled with the glory of the LORD. Because all those men which have seen my glory, and my miracles, which I did in Egypt and in the wilderness, and have tempted me now these ten times, and have not hearkened to my voice; surely they shall not see the land which I sware unto their fathers, neither shall any of them that provoked me see it. But my servant Caleb, because he had another spirit with him, and hath followed me fully, him will I bring into the land whereinto he went; and his seed shall possess it.

(Numbers 14:20–24 KJV)

By his positive confession, Caleb settled his destiny for the positive.

Numbers 14:26–32 continues:

And the LORD spake unto Moses and unto Aaron, saying, How long shall I bear with this evil congregation, which murmur against me? I have heard the murmurings of the children of Israel, which they murmur against me. Say unto them, As truly as I live, saith the LORD, as ye have spoken in mine ears, so will I do to you: your carcasses shall fall in this wilderness; and all that were numbered of you, according to your whole number, from twenty years old and upward, which have murmured against me, doubtless ye shall not come into the land, concerning which I sware to make you dwell therein, save Caleb the son of Jephunneh, and Joshua the son of Nun. But your little ones, which ye said should be a prey, them will I bring in, and they shall know the land which ye have despised. But as for you, your carcasses, they shall fall in this wilderness. (KJV)

Notice the words, *"As you have spoken in my ears, so will I do to you."* God is saying, in effect, "You have settled what I will do to you by the words that you have spoken."

And the men, which Moses sent to search the land, who returned, and made all the congregation to murmur against him, by bringing up a slander upon the land, even those men that did bring up the evil report upon the land, died by the plague before the LORD. [They settled their own deaths. They spoke words of death, and death was the outcome.] *But Joshua the son of Nun, and*

Caleb the son of Jephunneh, which were of the men that went to search the land, lived still. (Numbers 14:36–38 KJV)

Death and life are in the power of the tongue. How much more clearly could that be illustrated? The men that spoke negatively settled for death. The men that spoke positively received life. They settled their own destinies by what they spoke. The ones that said, "We are not able," *were not* able. The ones that said, "We are able," *were* able.

In the New Testament, our experience as Christians is directly compared to that of Israel in the Old Testament. We are warned that the same lessons apply to us. Hebrews 4:1–2 reads:

Therefore, since the promise of entering his rest still stands, let us be careful that none of you be found to have fallen short of it. For we also have had the gospel [the Good News] *preached to us, just as they did; but the message they heard was of no value to them, because those who heard it did not combine it with faith.* (NIV)

The same promise that God gave to Israel

still stands for us a promise of entering into the rest of God, but we must be careful that we do not fall short of it in the same way that they did in the Old Testament. Their problem was they heard the message, a promise from God, but they added that one fatal word *"nevertheless."* Instead of focusing on the promise of God and boldly confessing their faith in God's promise and power, they focused on the negative. They looked at the giants and the walled cities and said, "We are not able." Thank God for two men who had the faith and the courage to say, *"We are well able."*

When you face God's promise concerning a certain situation, what are you going to do with your tongue? Are you going to give assent to the promise of God? Are you going to identify yourself with the promise of God and say, "God said it; I'm able." Or are you going to be one of those who say, "Nevertheless, look at all the problems. God said it, but somehow I don't feel able"? Remember, just as those spies settled their destinies with their tongues by the words that they spoke, so the same lesson applies to whoever has heard the gospel. We likewise settle our destinies by the words that we speak.

Ten of the twelve spies focused on the problems, not on the promises. Two of the twelve spies, Joshua and Caleb, focused on the promises, not on the problems. Joshua and Caleb said, *"We are well able."* The other spies said, "We are not able." Each got exactly what they said. They all settled their own destinies by the way they used their tongues.

Chapter Five

Diseases of the Tongue

We have studied an example from the Old Testament that illustrates how *"death and life are in the power of the tongue."* We learned that the right use of the tongue will impart life, and, conversely, the wrong use will impart death.

Now we will consider certain specific diseases that affect our tongues. These six diseases that commonly infect our lives through the misuse of our tongues can, in some cases, be fatal if left unchecked.

Disease Number One:

Excessive Talking

This disease is so common that people

accept it as normal when it is not.

When words are many, sin is not absent,
but he who holds his tongue is wise.

(Proverbs 10:19 NIV)

Another version of the same Scripture verse reads:

When there are many words, transgression
is unavoidable, but he who restrains his
lips is wise. (NAS)

In other words, if you say too much, you are bound to say something wrong. There is no alternative.

We are also warned in the Bible not to use too many words toward God Himself. This is a warning that most of us really need to hear. This admonition is found in Ecclesiastes:

Guard your steps when you go to the house
of God. Go near to listen rather than to
offer the sacrifice of fools, who do not know
that they do wrong. Do not be quick with
your mouth, do not be hasty in your heart
to utter anything before God. God is in
heaven and you are on earth, so let your
words be few. (Ecclesiastes 5:1–2 NIV)

Somebody said to me once, "Remember, it's just as much a sin to *sing* a lie as it is to *tell* a lie." I have heard people sing hymns of total consecration and surrender to God, such as, "All to Jesus, I surrender." Then, when the offering plate comes around, they drop in a quarter. The two actions are not consistent. If you are not going to give your life to God, do not tell Him that you are surrendering all, because God is going to hold you to account for the words you speak (or sing) in His presence.

A little further on in the same chapter, the Scripture indicates that an angel records what we say when we are speaking, praying or worshiping. One day we are going to be confronted by that angel and the record of what we have said. Then, the Bible says, it will be too late to say, "I didn't really mean it," because we will be held accountable for all we have said, sung, or prayed. One day those words are going to be held up before us, and we are going to have to answer for them if we have been insincere and have not really lived according to the things we have said.

The next verse, in Ecclesiastes, continues:

As a dream comes when there are many cares, so the speech of a fool when there are many words. (Ecclesiastes 5:3 NIV)

To use too many words is the mark of a fool. The King James Version of Ecclesiastes 5:3 is even more blunt:

For a dream cometh through the multitude of business; and a fool's voice is known by multitude of words.

When you hear a person continually talking, you need no other evidence: that person is a fool. *"A fool's voice is known by a multitude of words."* What is the root problem? I believe it is restlessness. Compare that to what James says in James 3:8:

No man can tame the tongue. It is a restless evil, full of deadly poison. (NIV)

People who are always talking are restless people, and our contemporary culture is filled with them. Have you ever been with somebody who made your head swim by all the words that came out of his or her mouth? What is the root problem? Restlessness. Excessive talking is a sure indication of someone whose heart is not at rest.

Disease Number Two:

Idle or Careless Words

In Matthew 12:36, Jesus says this:

But I tell you that men will have to give account on the day of judgment for every careless word they have spoken. (NIV)

One day we are going to have to answer for every word we have spoken. We are going to have to answer for words that were idle, insincere, that we did not really mean, that we were not prepared to stand behind, or that were not worked out in our lives.

In the Sermon on the Mount, recorded in Matthew 5:37, Jesus states:

Simply let your "Yes" be "Yes," and your "No," "No"; anything beyond this comes from the evil one. (NIV)

That is an astonishing statement. If we say more than we mean, then the exaggeration (unnecessary emphasis or overdoing) in our speech comes from the evil one.

Let me sum it up in just one simple word of advice. *If you don't mean it, don't say it.* If you will follow that one rule, I promise you, it will change your whole life. You will be a different person. If you would keep that rule for one year, I promise you that a year from now you will be a different and a much better person.

Disease Number Three:

Gossip

Do not go about spreading slander among your people.   (Leviticus 19:16 NIV)

Going about spreading slander—idle, untrue, exaggerated, malicious talk—is gossip. The very title of Satan in the New Testament, the word rendered *"devil,"* means "a slanderer" in Greek. That is its root meaning and the main description of Satan in the Bible. If you gossip or tell tales, you are actually doing the devil's work for him. You are a representative of Satan. Not only must we be careful not to give out gossip, we have a responsibility not to receive gossip also.

The words of a gossip are like choice morsels; they go down to a man's inmost parts   (Proverbs 18:8 NIV)

How true that is of human nature. When

we hear something about someone that is bad or shows them in a bad light, something in the human heart rejoices. *"The words of a gossip are like choice morsels."* Be careful when one of those choice morsels of gossip is placed in front of you that you do not swallow it. They are poisoned. They taste sweet but they poison us. And, as we receive them into our hearts, our lives will become poisoned by those morsels of gossip.

A gossip betrays a confidence; so avoid a man who talks too much.

(Proverbs 20:19 NIV)

See how closely these various diseases are related. If you listen to a gossip, you become "an accessory after the fact." If you receive somebody who has stolen something and accept those stolen goods from them, then in legal terms you become an accessory after the fact. So, if you entertain a gossip and listen to his words, you become an accessory to the gossip. This is what God says in Psalm 15:

O LORD, who may abide in Thy tent? Who may dwell on Thy holy hill? He who walks with integrity, and works righteousness,

*and speaks truth in his heart. He does not
slander with his tongue, nor does evil to his
neighbor, nor takes up a reproach against
his friend.* (Psalm 15:1–3 NAS)

There are various requirements for access
to God's presence, in order to *"dwell on His
holy hill."* We must walk with integrity; we
must work righteousness; we must speak the
truth in our hearts.

Then three things we must not do are
listed. We must not slander with our tongues,
and we must not do evil to our neighbor. Also,
we must not take up a reproach, or receive a
reproach, against our friends.

It is not enough that we do not slander; we
must not receive the slanderer. We must not
take up a reproach against someone whom we
know. We must not eat those choice morsels of
the gossip because they are poison, and many
relationships are poisoned by eating them.

Disease Number Four:

Lying

We need to be careful that we use the
right word to describe this disease of the

tongue. Somebody has used the phrase, "evang–**e-l-a-s-t-i-c**–ally speaking." The evangelist sees 200 people come forward in his crusade and by the time the report is in his newsletter, it is 500. What is that— exaggeration or lying? It is really lying. I do not mention this to be critical of others. It is important that every one of us be very careful that we are not found guilty of lying.

In Proverbs 6:16–19, the writer tells of seven things that the Lord hates. Hate is a very strong word. This is what it says:

> *There are six things the LORD hates, seven that are detestable to him: haughty eyes, a lying tongue, hands that shed innocent blood, a heart that devises wicked schemes, feet that are quick to rush into evil, a false witness who pours out lies and a man who stirs up dissension among brothers.* (NIV)

Out of those seven specific things that the Lord hates, there are three that are related to the tongue: first, *"a lying tongue"*; second, *"a false witness"* (obviously that affects the tongue also); third, *"a man who stirs up dissension among brothers"* (and normally the way that dissension is stirred up is by words). So out of seven things that the Lord hates, there are three that affect the tongue, and of those three, two are specifically connected with lying. This is stated again in Proverbs 12:22:

> *The LORD detests lying lips, but he delights in men who are truthful.* (NIV)

In that verse we have two sets of opposites. We have the word "detest" and the word "delight." *"The LORD detests lying lips, but he delights in men who are truthful."* There is nothing in between.

Then we have the other two opposites, "lying" and "truthful." Again, there is nothing in between. If it is not truthful, it is a lie. If it is a lie, the Lord detests it. If it is truthful, the Lord delights in it.

Our problem is that we have so many gray areas in our thinking. But I question whether those gray areas are found in Scripture. If traced to its source, every lie comes from the devil. That is a frightening thought, but I will back it up with the words of Jesus Himself. Speaking to the religious leaders of His day (and bear in mind, they were *very* religious people), Jesus said:

> *You belong to your father, the devil, and you want to carry out your father's desire. He was a murderer from the beginning, not holding to the truth, for there is no truth in him. When he lies, he speaks his native language, for he is a liar and the father of lies.*   (John 8:44 NIV)

Every time a lie passes through our lips, it comes from the devil.

One more very important, frightening fact about the disease of lying is that unless the disease is arrested and healed, it is fatal.

> *But the cowardly, the unbelieving, the vile, the murderers, the sexually immoral, those who practice magic arts, the idolaters and all liars—their place will be in the fiery lake of burning sulfur. This is the second death.*   (Revelation 21:8 NIV)

Notice the groups of people: *"the cowardly, the unbelieving, the vile, the murderers, the sexually immoral, those who practice magic arts, the idolaters, and all liars."* That disease is incurable. There is no way out: *"their place will be in the fiery lake of burning sulfur."* Once a person is consigned to that second death, it is ultimate. I repeat what I said: Unless this disease of lying is arrested and healed, it is sure to be fatal!

Revelation 22:15 speaks about the city of God:

> *Outside are the dogs, those who practice magic arts, the sexually immoral, the murderers, the idolaters and everyone who loves and practices falsehood* [or lies]. (NIV)

So each of us must determine: Am I willing to be healed of this disease of lying, *or am I prepared to lose my soul forever?* Unless arrested and healed, the disease of lying is ultimately fatal.

Disease Number Five:

Flattery

> *Help, LORD, for the godly are no more; the faithful have vanished from among men. Everyone lies to his neighbor; their flattering lips speak with deception. May*

the LORD cut off all flattering lips and every boastful tongue. (Psalm 12:1–3 NIV)

In this Scripture, David is speaking about a state of moral decline in the human race. I believe it is not unlike what we see around us today. Godly men are difficult to find. The faithful have vanished. What is the result? *"Everyone lies to his neighbor; their flattering lips speak with deception."* A judgment of God is pronounced by the Scripture upon these flattering lips: *"May the LORD cut off all flattering lips and every boastful tongue."*

In Proverbs 26:28, we are warned:

A lying tongue hates those it hurts, and a flattering mouth works ruin. (NIV)

If we listen to and receive flattery, or if we become flatterers, the end is ruin.

Whoever flatters his neighbor is spreading a net for his feet. (Proverbs 29:5 NIV)

After many years in the ministry, I have learned by practical experience that this is true. There are people who will speak flattering words, but they are not sincere. There is another motive behind it. And many times, if it had not been the grace of God, my feet would have been caught in that net of flattery. I would have been led into some commitment or some relationship that was outside the will of God. So bear that in mind, *"a flattering mouth works ruin,"* and, *"whoever flatters his neighbor is spreading a net for his feet."*

Disease Number Six:

Hastiness of Speech

Do you see a man who is hasty in his words?
There is more hope for a fool than for him.
(Proverbs 29:20 NAS)

This verse says if we are hasty in our words, our condition is worse than that of a fool. That is a solemn statement because the Bible has nothing good to say about the fool.

There is one example in Scripture of a man who was hasty in his words *just once* and tells of the price it cost him. The man was Moses. He was told by God to go ahead of the children of Israel, speak to a rock, and it would bring forth water. But he was so angry with the children of Israel that he said to them, *"You rebels, must we bring you water out of this rock?"* Then, instead of speaking to the rock, he smote it. (See Numbers 20:7–12.) That act of disobedience, expressed in hasty words, cost him the privilege of leading the children of Israel into the Promised Land. This is described in Psalm 106:32–33:

➤ *They* [the children of Israel] *angered him* [Moses] *also at the waters of strife, so that it went ill with Moses for their sakes: because they provoked his spirit, so that he spake unadvisedly with his lips.* (KJV)

Notice the diagnosis. A provoked spirit causes us to speak unadvisedly with our lips, and these hasty words cost us many privileges and blessings. If Moses had to pay that price for that *one* hasty statement, let us beware that we do not also say things hastily which will cost us dearly in the spiritual realm.

Chapter Six

The Root of the Problem

God has made a provision in Scripture for the healing of our tongues. The first step in acquiring this is to identify the root of the problem. The testimony of Scripture is clear and unequivocal: *the root of every problem affecting our tongues is in our hearts.*

In Matthew, Jesus says:

Make a tree good and its fruit will be good, or make a tree bad and its fruit will be bad, for a tree is recognized by its fruit. You brood of vipers, how can you who are evil say anything good? For out of the overflow of the heart the mouth speaks. The good man brings good things out of the good stored up in him, and the evil man brings evil things out of the evil stored up in him. ✤(Matthew 12:33–35 NIV)

The heart is the tree and the words are the fruit. The words that come out of the mouth indicate the condition of the heart. If the heart is good, the words will be good. If the heart is evil, the words will be evil. Our hearts are either good or evil all the way through. Whatever flows out of your mouth indicates the contents of your heart.

If you accidentally spill some water from a pail onto the kitchen floor and see that the water you spilled is dirty and greasy, you do not need to examine the water that is left in the bucket. You know it is dirty and greasy. The same applies to our hearts. If evil, impure, unbelieving, corrupt words come out of our mouths, then that indicates the same condition prevails in our hearts.

Compare the text from Matthew with James 3:9–12, where James speaks about the inconsistencies of religious people:

With the tongue we praise our Lord and Father, and with it we curse men, who

*have been made in God's likeness. Out of
the same mouth come praise* [or blessing]
*and cursing. My brothers, this should not
be. Can both fresh water and salt water
flow from the same spring? My brothers,
can a fig tree bear olives, or a grapevine
bear figs? Neither can a salt spring produce
fresh water.* (NIV)

James combines two pictures there. The
one is of a spring of water; the other is of a
tree. He says that an olive tree will never bear
another kind of fruit, such as figs. The kind of
tree indicates the kind of fruit. James is using
the same picture as Jesus. The tree is the heart
and the fruit is the words that come out of the
mouth. He also uses another picture, a spring
of water. He says that if brackish, salty water
comes out of a spring, you know the water in
the spring is brackish and salty.

These two pictures are parallel but not
identical. The two trees represent two natures.
The corrupt tree is the old man or the old
person. The good tree is the new man in Jesus
Christ. The old man cannot bring forth good
fruit. Jesus said that clearly many times. Out
of that old, carnal nature will always come

fruit that corresponds to that nature.

The fountain, or the spring, represents something spiritual. A pure spring is the Holy Spirit. A corrupt, brackish, salty, impure spring is another spirit.

Therefore, we have two potential problems indicated by the mouth: first, the old, corrupt nature which has not been changed goes on producing corrupt fruit; and second, some kind of spirit, which is not the Holy Spirit, brings forth impure, brackish water. The essence of the teaching is the same in both: that which is inside us, the condition of our hearts, determines what comes out of our mouths. So the problem of the tongue takes us back inevitably to the problem of the heart.

We are confronted by the truth that Solomon spoke in Proverbs 4:23:

> *Above all else, guard your heart, for it is the* > *wellspring of life.* (NIV)

The word *"wellspring"* agrees with the picture that James used of a fountain or a spring that brings forth the kind of water that is characteristic of that spring. Another translation of Proverbs 4:23 says:

*Watch over your heart with all diligence,
for from it flow the springs of life.* (NAS)

Whatever flows out in your life or through your mouth originates in your heart. If the source is pure, that which comes out will be pure. If the source is corrupt, that which comes out will be corrupt.

With this, we can compare the words of Hebrews 12:15–16:

*See to it that no one comes short of the grace
of God; that no root of bitterness springing
up causes trouble, and by it many be defiled;
that there be no immoral or godless person
like Esau, who sold his own birthright for
a single meal.* (NAS)

Esau was entitled to the birthright, but he sold it and lost it. We can have a birthright or a promise from God, but if we do not conduct ourselves rightly, we will lose our birthright and our inheritance just like the ten spies who came with the negative report.

The reason why Esau acted like that is traced back to a root of bitterness in his heart. He was bitter against his brother Jacob. This root of bitterness in his heart brought forth bitter fruit in his life which corrupted his life and caused him to lose his birthright. (See Genesis 25:19–34.) Therefore, the root of the problem was in his heart.

The Scripture warns us that if there is a root of bitterness in the heart of any one of us, others may be defiled by it. The corrupt, negative use of the tongue is infectious. The ten spies came back with a negative report. They corrupted the *whole nation*. The whole nation was infected with that negative disease. That is one reason why God treats it so seriously. It is an infectious disease.

There are other examples of evil roots in our hearts that express themselves through our tongues and cause problems which rob us of the blessings that God desires us to have. We can have roots of resentment, unbelief, impurity, or pride. Whatever the nature of the root in our hearts, it will manifest itself in the way we speak. We may want to be gracious and kind, but a root of resentment will poison our words with a kind of resentful spirit. We will try to say nice things, but they will not come out right. We may claim to be believers, but a root of unbelief will cause us to do as the ten spies and add our *"nevertheless"* to God's promises. The same is true of impurity and pride.

Let me remind you of the story about the doctor in the desert checking his dysentery patients. The first question was, "Good morning, how are you?" But he did not really care much about the answer to that question. The second request was, "Show me your tongue." How would you respond if God said to you, "Show Me your tongue"?

Chapter Seven

First Steps to Healing

Let us look at three simple, practical, scriptural steps to dealing with the problem of your tongue.

Step Number 1:

⁶ *Call Your Problem by Its Right Name: Sin.*

It is important that we become honest. As long as we use some fancy, psychological terminology to cover, condone, excuse or pretend that our problem is not really there, nothing will happen. We must come to the moment of honesty. I have seen this many times in God's dealings, both with me and with many other people. When we come to the moment of truth, God moves in and helps us. As long as we try to excuse, cover up or misrepresent our problem, God does nothing for us. Sometimes we say, "God, why don't You help me?" God replies (we may not hear Him, but God replies), "I'm waiting for you to be honest—honest with yourself and honest with Me."

That is the first and the most important step. Once you take that step, you are well on the way to the steps that follow. Call your problem by its right name: sin.*

Religious people have many different ways of excusing or glossing over the misuse of our tongues. We think it does not matter much what we say, but God says it makes all the difference. In fact, we have seen that you settle your destiny by what you say. Jesus said, *"By your words you shall be justified, by your words you shall be condemned"* (Matthew 12:37). It is a serious matter. Do not trifle with it. Come to the moment of truth and say, "I have a problem: it is sin." When you have come there, you are ready to take the second step.

Step Number 2:

Confess Your Sin and Receive Forgiveness and Cleansing.

First John 1:7–9 illustrates this clearly:

If we walk in the light as He Himself is in the light, we have fellowship with one another, and the blood of Jesus His Son cleanses us from all sin. If we say that we have no sin, we are deceiving ourselves, and the truth is not in us. If we confess our sins, He is faithful and righteous to forgive us our sins and to cleanse us from all unrighteousness. (NAS)

Again, we see the importance of being honest. The blood of Jesus does not cleanse in the dark. Only when we come to the light can we receive the cleansing of the blood of Jesus. If we are walking in the light, the blood of Jesus Christ continually cleanses us and keeps us pure from all sin. If we say that we have no sin, which I have pointed out to be the real problem, we are deceiving ourselves. The truth is not in us and we are not in the light. We are still in the dark where God's provision does not work.

Then we come to the alternative. If we confess our sins, come to the light, and acknowledge the real nature and the seriousness of our problem, then God *"is faithful and righteous to forgive us our sins and to cleanse us from all unrighteousness."* Two words are used, *"faithful"* and *"righteous."* God is faithful because He has promised, and He will keep His promise. God is righteous or just because Jesus has already paid the penalty for our sins; therefore, He can forgive us without compromising His justice.

If we confess our sins, the guarantee of Scripture is that God in faithfulness and in justice will forgive us our sins and cleanse us from all unrighteousness. God not only forgives but, even more important, He cleanses. Once our hearts are cleansed, because the heart is the wellspring of life, we do not go on committing the same sins.

If you believe that your sins are forgiven but you find experientially that you have not been cleansed, I would like to question whether you have really been forgiven. The same God who forgives also cleanses. The same Scripture that promises forgiveness also promises cleansing. God never stops halfway. If we meet the conditions, we get the whole packet. If we do not meet the conditions, we do not get half, we get nothing. If we confess our sins, God is faithful and righteous to forgive us our sins and to cleanse us from all unrighteousness. Once our hearts are cleansed, then the problem will not be there. Remember, the condition of the heart determines what comes out of the mouth. A clean heart cannot produce unclean utterances. Unclean utterances indicate an unclean heart.

First, if we come to the light, confess, and turn to God with the problem, then God is faithful and righteous to forgive. The record of the past is blotted out, and all those things you wish you had never said are blotted out. Secondly, God cleanses your heart. Then, out of a clean, pure heart, what comes through your lips will be clean and pure. If your heart glorifies God, then your lips will glorify God. God solves the problem of the tongue and of the lips by dealing with the condition of the heart.

Step Number 3:

Refuse Sin; Yield to God.

There is a negative and a positive which go together like the two opposite sides of the same coin. You must exercise your will both ways. You must say "no" to sin and "yes" to God. You *must* do both. You cannot say "no" to sin without saying "yes" to God, because you will be in a vacuum which will be filled again with the same problem. You cannot escape from sin without yielding to God.

In Romans 6:12–14, Paul says:

Therefore do not let sin reign in your mortal body that you should obey its lusts, and do not go on presenting the members of your body to sin as instruments of unrighteousness; but present yourselves to God as those alive from the dead, and your members [or the parts of your body] *as instruments of righteousness to God. For sin shall not be master over you, for you are not under law, but under grace.* (NAS)

When sin challenges you, say, "No, I will not yield to you; I will not yield the parts of my body. Above all, I will not yield that member which causes most of the trouble: my tongue. Sin, you cannot control my tongue any longer."

Then turn to God and say, "God, I yield my tongue to You, and I ask You to control the member which I cannot control."

Let us look at what James says:

For every species of beasts and birds, of reptiles and creatures of the sea, is tamed, and has been tamed by the human race. But no one can tame the tongue; it is a restless evil and full of deadly poison.
(James 3:7–8 NAS)

You must accept the fact that you cannot tame or control your own tongue. Only one power can control your tongue for good: the power of God through the Holy Spirit. When you have been forgiven and cleansed and then are challenged again to use your tongue sinfully, you must say to sin, "You cannot have my tongue; I refuse it to you." Then you must say to the Holy Spirit, "Holy Spirit, I yield my tongue to You. I cannot control my tongue. I ask You to control my tongue for me."

Let us just briefly review those three steps. First, call your problem by its right name—call it sin. Second, confess your sin, and receive forgiveness and cleansing. Third, refuse to yield to sin; determine to yield to God. That is the climax of the process of deliverance and of healing. It is yielding to God the Holy Spirit that member which you can never control.

Chapter Eight

The Reason You Have
a Tongue

We have already seen that the root of every problem affecting our tongues is in our hearts. Obviously, this means that in order to deal with problems affecting our tongues we must first deal with the root problems in our hearts.

We considered the three steps we must take to deal with these root problems in our hearts that are manifested through our tongues. First, call your problem by its right name which is sin. Come to the moment of truth. God will only deal with you on the basis of truth. God is the God of truth. The Holy Spirit is the Spirit of truth.

Second, confess and receive forgiveness

and cleansing on the basis of the promise in 1 John 1:9:

> *If we confess our sins,* [God] *is faithful and righteous to forgive us our sins and to cleanse us from all unrighteousness.* (NAS)

God not only forgives the past, He cleanses the heart so that the problem itself is dealt with at the root. Then there is a change in the fruit that comes out of the heart.

Third, refuse sin, and yield to God. Say "no" to sin and "yes" to God. Refuse sin, and yield to the Holy Spirit. The only power in the universe that can control your tongue effectively for good is the Holy Spirit.

Let us deal more fully with the positive aspect of this third step: yielding our tongues to God.

First, we need to understand the real reason why the Creator gave each of us a mouth with a tongue in it. There is an answer to this in Scripture but it is one of those interesting examples of truth in Scripture which can only be found by comparing two passages of Scripture and setting them side by side. As we do this, there comes a revelation which is not given to us solely in one of the two passages.

In this case, the two passages that I have in mind are taken from the Old and New Testaments. In the New Testament the Old Testament passage is quoted in a way which brings out a meaning that is not apparent in the Old Testament. The Old Testament passage is Psalm 16:8–9:

I have set the LORD continually before me; because He is at my right hand, I will not be shaken. Therefore my heart is glad, and my glory rejoices; my flesh also will dwell securely. (NAS)

Please focus on the phrase, *"my glory rejoices."* On the day of Pentecost, when the Spirit of God fell and the crowd gathered to know the reason, Peter preached his famous sermon. He referred to everything that happened in the life, the death, and the resurrection of Jesus. He quoted various passages from the Old Testament to prove that Jesus was indeed the Messiah and the Son of God. One of the passages he quoted was the one in Psalm 16:8–9. The quotation is found in Acts 2:25–26, where Peter says this:

> *For David says of Him, "I was always beholding the Lord in my presence; For He is at my right hand, that I may not be shaken. Therefore my heart was glad and my tongue exulted; Moreover my flesh also will abide in hope."* (NAS)

Now, we put together these two key phrases: Psalm 16:9, *"my glory rejoices"*; and Acts 2:26, quoting the same passage, *"my tongue exulted."* Where David says in the Psalm *"my glory"*; Peter, inspired and interpreted by the Holy Spirit, says *"my tongue."* This tells us something very profound and important: *our tongues are our glory.* You might ask why. The answer is because the Creator gave each of us a tongue for one supreme purpose—to glorify Him. The only reason for a tongue is that with it you and I may glorify God. That is why our tongues become our glory. It is the member by which, above all others, we may glorify the Creator. This leads to a consequence of great importance. Every use of our tongue that does not glorify God is a misuse because we were given our tongues to glorify God.

We can look at that well-known statement of Paul in Romans 3:23:

For all have sinned and fall short of the glory of God. (NAS)

The essence of sin is not necessarily committing some terrible crime. The essence of sin is falling short of the glory of God or not living for God's glory. People might argue with that and say, "It's not true of me; I have never fallen short of the glory of God."

But I ask you to check the use of your tongue. Remember, the only reason you have a tongue is to glorify God. Every use of your tongue that does not glorify God is a misuse. I do not believe that there is one of us that could honestly say that we have always used our tongues for the glory of God. Therefore, we must acknowledge the truth of Paul's statement that we have all sinned and fallen short of the glory of God. If this is not true in any other area, then it is true in the area of our tongues.

Two different kinds of fire meet on the human tongue. First, there is a fire from hell that inflames the tongue of the natural, unregenerate, sinful man. James says:

The tongue also is a fire, a world of evil among the parts of the body. It corrupts the whole person, sets the whole course of his life on fire, and is itself set on fire by hell.

(James 3:6 NIV)

This fire in the human tongue comes from hell itself, and its fruit—its results and consequences—are hellish. But on the day of Pentecost, when God brought into being the redeemed community that He wanted to use for His glory in the earth, another kind of fire came from another source. The fire of the Holy Spirit came from heaven, not from hell. It first operated in the tongues of those in the Upper Room. In other words, the fire of God from heaven drove out the natural tongue's fire of hell. The fire from hell was replaced by a fire that cleanses, purifies and glorifies God. Consider Acts 2:1–4:

When the day of Pentecost came, they were all together in one place. Suddenly a sound like the blowing of a violent wind came from heaven and filled the whole house where they were sitting. They saw what seemed to be tongues of fire that separated and came to rest on each of them. [Note that there was a tongue of fire for each one.] *All of them were filled with the Holy Spirit and began to speak in other tongues as the Spirit enabled them.* (NIV)

Notice the Spirit operated first in their tongues. The fire of God from heaven gave them a new way to use their tongues. Then the Scripture makes it plain that everything they said after that, through the Holy Spirit, glorified God. They were using their tongues for the purpose God had given them tongues.

The key to this problem is yielding our tongues to the Holy Spirit. This is clearly stated by Paul in Ephesians 5:17–18:

Hebrews 4:14

Therefore do not be foolish, but understand what the Lord's will is. [The next verse tells us the Lord's will:] *Do not get drunk on wine, which leads to debauchery. Instead, be filled with the Spirit.* (NIV)

We need to put those two things together. It is sinful to get drunk on wine, but it is also sinful not to be filled with the Holy Spirit. The positive commandment is just as valid as the negative. Do not be drunk with wine, but be filled with the Holy Spirit. In a sense, it is two different kinds of drunkenness, if you can accept that, because on the day of Pentecost, when the men and women were first filled with the Holy Spirit, the mockers said, "They're drunk." In a certain sense, they *were* inebriated, but with a totally different kind of inebriation. They were not drunk with wine, but they were filled with the Holy Spirit. Then Paul goes on:

> *Speak to one another with psalms, hymns, and spiritual songs. Sing and make music in your heart to the Lord, always giving thanks to God the Father for everything, in the name of our Lord Jesus Christ.*
> (Ephesians 5:19–20 NIV)

Notice the word *"speak"* that comes after the injunction *"be filled with the Holy Spirit."* There are fifteen places in the New Testament where it speaks about people being either filled with or full of the Holy Spirit. And in every place the initial manifestation came through the mouth. *"Out of the abundance of the heart, the mouth speaks."*

When you are filled with the Holy Spirit, the first manifestation will come out of your mouth, through your tongue. Instead of murmuring, complaining, criticizing, and giving vent to unbelief, Paul says that you will speak, sing, make music, and give thanks. The whole use of your tongue will be positive, not negative.

The solution to every problem of sin in our lives must be a positive one. It is not enough to give up sinning; we must have righteousness. It is not enough to deny your tongue to the devil; you must yield your tongue to the Holy Spirit. Be filled with the Holy Spirit and speak: that is the remedy.

Chapter Nine

The Importance of
Your Confession

We need to see how the right use of the tongue links us in a very special way to Jesus Christ as our High Priest. The high priesthood of Jesus is an eternal ministry which goes on continually in heaven. After He had dealt with our sins, died, risen again and ascended into heaven, He entered into a ministry as our High Priest forever, always representing us in God's presence. He is our High Priest on the condition that we make the right confession with our tongues.

This is what the writer of Hebrews says:

*Therefore, holy brethren, partakers of
a heavenly calling, consider Jesus, the*

Apostle and High Priest of our confession.
(Hebrews 3:1 NAS)

Note that last phrase. Jesus is the High Priest of our confession. It is our confession that links us to Jesus as High Priest. If we merely believe, but make no confession, then His high priesthood cannot operate on our behalf. It is on the basis of our spoken confession, not of our unspoken faith, that Jesus operates in heaven as our High Priest.

It is tremendously important that we make and maintain the right confession. The word *"confess"* means, literally, "to say the same thing as." In this usage, confession is saying the same thing with our mouths as God says in the Scripture. It is making the words of our mouths agree with the Word of God in the Scripture.

When we make the words of our mouths agree in faith with what God says in the Bible, then that enables Jesus to exercise His high priestly ministry as our representative in the presence of God. If we make the wrong confession, we frustrate His ministry. It depends on our making the right confession.

It is our confession that links us to Jesus as our High Priest. This is brought out twice more in Hebrews. The first reference is in Hebrews 4:14: *Ephesian 5:17-18*

> *Since then we have a great high priest who has passed through the heavens, Jesus the Son of God, let us hold fast our confession.* Page 81 (NAS)

It is our confession that continues to link us to Jesus as our High Priest. And again, we read in Hebrews:

> *And since we have a great [high] priest over the house of God,....Let us hold fast the confession of our hope without wavering, for He who promised is faithful.*
>
> (Hebrews 10:21, 23 NAS)

Every time the Bible speaks about Jesus as our High Priest, it says we must make, maintain, and hold fast the confession of our faith and our hope. It is our confession that links us to Jesus as our High Priest. If we do not maintain that confession, we frustrate His ministry on our behalf. Right confession is actually essential for salvation.

The word is nigh thee, even in thy mouth, and in thy heart: that is, the word of faith, which we preach; that if thou shalt confess with thy mouth the Lord Jesus, and shalt believe in thine heart that God hath raised him from the dead, thou shalt be saved. For with the heart man believeth unto righteousness; and with the mouth confession is made unto salvation.

(Romans 10:8–10 KJV)

Again, as we have seen all the way through, there is a direct link between the heart and the mouth. Jesus said, *"Out of the overflow of the heart, the mouth speaks."* Salvation depends on two things: exercising faith in our hearts and making the right confession with our mouths.

In the Bible *"salvation"* is the great all-inclusive word for all the blessings and provisions of God that have been obtained for us through the death of Jesus Christ. It includes spiritual, physical, financial, temporal, and eternal blessings. All those blessings purchased by the death of Jesus are summed up in the word *"salvation."*

cool

To enter into the fullness of God's salvation in every area of our lives, we have to make the right confession. In every area, whatever it may be, we must say the same with our mouths as God says in His Word. When our confession agrees with the Word of God, we are moving into the full provision of God in salvation, and we have the ministry of Jesus as our High Priest operative on our behalf in heaven. With Him standing behind us on the basis of our confession, there is nothing that can hinder us or keep us from moving on into the fullness of our salvation. Our confession links us to Jesus as our High Priest. That is why what we say with our mouths determines our experience.

Let us return briefly to the illustration of the tongue as the rudder of the human life.

Or take ships as an example. Although they are so large and are driven by strong winds, they are steered by a very small rudder wherever the pilot wants to go. Likewise the tongue is a small part of the body.

(James 3:4–5 NIV)

What the rudder is to the ship, the tongue

is to the body or to the life. The right use of the rudder directs the ship properly. The wrong use brings shipwreck. The same is true with the tongue. The right use of the tongue brings success and salvation in its fullness. The wrong use brings shipwreck and failure.

The ship is steered with a very small rudder wherever the pilot wants to go. A great ocean liner may have a captain with many years of experience, but when he comes into a harbor, he is not permitted to berth that ship himself. It is an almost unvarying rule that the captain must take a pilot on board and allow the pilot to assume responsibility for the use of the rudder and the berthing of the ship.

You and I may feel we are capable of handling our lives, but there are situations where we cannot manage. We must take a pilot on board and let him assume responsibility. Can you guess who the pilot is? Of course! The pilot is the Holy Spirit. Only the Holy Spirit can enable us always to use our tongues rightly and to make the right confession.

The Holy Spirit is the Spirit of truth and the Spirit of faith. When He motivates and controls our words and speech, they become positive. Our speech then honors God and brings the blessings of God into our lives. Every one of us needs the Holy Spirit to pilot our lives by controlling our tongues. He is the ultimate solution to the problem of the human tongue.

God permits us to come to a place of failure. He says, "None of you can control your own tongue." And then He says, "But I have a Pilot. Will you invite the Pilot on board?" All you need to do is simply respond with a prayer such as this:

Holy Spirit, I really cannot control my tongue aright. Come in and take control. I yield to You. Give me a tongue that glorifies God. Amen.

About the Author

Derek Prince (1915–2003) was born in Bangalore, India, into a British military family. He was educated as a scholar of classical languages (Greek, Latin, Hebrew, and Aramaic) at Eton College and Cambridge University in England and later at Hebrew University, Israel. As a student, he was a philosopher and self-proclaimed atheist. He held a fellowship (equivalent to a professorship) in Ancient and Modern Philosophy at King's College, Cambridge.

While in the British Medical Corps during World War II, Prince began to study the Bible as a philosophical work. Converted through a powerful encounter with Jesus Christ, he was baptized in the Holy Spirit a few days later. This life-changing experience altered the whole course of his life, which he thereafter devoted to studying and teaching the Bible as the Word of God.

Discharged from the army in Jerusalem in 1945, he married Lydia Christensen, founder of a children's home there. Upon their marriage, he immediately became father to Lydia's eight adopted daughters—six Jewish, one Palestinian Arab, one English. Together the family saw the rebirth of the state of Israel in 1948. In the late 1950s the Princes adopted another daughter while he was serving as principal of a college in Kenya.

In 1963, the Princes immigrated to the United States and pastored a church in Seattle. Stirred by the tragedy of John F. Kennedy's assassination, he began to teach Americans how to intercede for their nation. In 1973, he became one of the founders of Intercessors for America. His book *Shaping History through Prayer and Fasting* has awakened Christians around the world to their responsibility to pray for their governments. Many consider underground translations of the book as instrumental in the fall of communist regimes in the former USSR, East Germany, and Czechoslovakia.

Lydia Prince died in 1975, and Derek married Ruth Baker (a single mother to three adopted children) in 1978. He met his second wife, like his first, while he was serving the Lord in Jerusalem. Ruth died in December

1998 in Jerusalem, where they had lived since 1981.

Until a few years before his own death in 2003 at the age of eighty-eight, Prince persisted in the ministry God had called him to as he traveled the world, imparting God's revealed truth, praying for the sick and afflicted, and sharing his prophetic insights into world events in the light of Scripture. He pioneered teaching on such groundbreaking themes as generational curses, the biblical significance of Israel, and demonology.

He is the author of more than fifty books, six hundred audio teachings, and one hundred video teachings, many of which have been translated and published in more than one hundred languages. His radio program, now known as *Derek Prince Legacy Radio*, began in 1979 and has been translated into over a dozen languages. Derek's main gift of explaining the Bible and its teaching in a clear, simple way has helped build a foundation of faith in millions of lives. His nondenominational, nonsectarian approach has made his teaching equally relevant and helpful to people from all racial and religious backgrounds, and his teaching is estimated to have reached more than half the globe.

Internationally recognized as a Bible scholar and spiritual patriarch, Derek Prince established a teaching ministry that spanned six continents and more than sixty years. In 2002, he said, "It is my desire—and I believe the Lord's desire—that this ministry continue the work, which God began through me over sixty years ago, until Jesus returns."

With its international headquarters in Charlotte, North Carolina, Derek Prince Ministries continues to reach out to believers in over 140 countries with Derek's teaching, fulfilling the mandate to keep on "until Jesus returns." This is accomplished through the outreaches of more than thirty Derek Prince Ministries International offices around the world, including primary work in Australia, Canada, China, France, Germany, the Netherlands, New Zealand, Norway, Russia, South Africa, Switzerland, the United Kingdom, and the United States. For current information about these and other worldwide locations, visit www.derekprince.org.